High School Dropout to Teacher of the Year

My Journey to Johnsonville:

The Collaborative Learning Community

By

Anthony Johnson, Jr.

And we know that all things work together for

good to them that love God, to them who are

the called according to his purpose.

Romans 8:28

Dedication

This book is dedicated to my mom, Dora Woodard; dad, Anthony Johnson, Sr.; grandmother, Augustine Ellis; mother-in-law Jessieca Lewis; and aunt, Carol Pierce. I work hard every day with my students to make you all proud.

Thank you, my beautiful wife and main supporter Desiree Johnson. Without your love, I would not be where I am today! Thanks to my three awesome daughters Jessieca, Adanya, and Kailah. Daddy is proud of the young ladies you all have grown into.

CONTENTS

Foreword

By Samantha L. Dias-Lacy, Ed.D.

Transforming the lives of others is a selfless act many unconsciously perform daily. Not to mention that changing the lives of others is no easy feat, especially when you feel isolated and work within a vacuum. When the odds are stacked against you, you have no choice but to persevere. For some, obstacles weaken the very core of an individual's soul and damage the very essence of who they are as a person. For others, obstacles are the very seeds needed to inspire and motivate new ideas and transformational experiences. Hence, they embrace challenges to brainstorm and identify multiple solutions to design opportunities that redefine the way people think and live their lives. Educators tend to be *those* individuals who positively revolutionize the way children think and engage in their own educational processes.

It is no secret that education policy in the United States today focuses on standardized assessments, teacher evaluations, and rigorous state standards. As a result of these unsubstantiated educational practices, there have been negative implications on instructional pedagogies and academic liberties. Moreover, some educator's express feelings of being stifled and restricted, unable to develop a learning environment that fosters creativity. On the other hand, there are educators who are risk takers, the outliers, who go against the grain and are not apprehensive about providing their students with the education that they deserve and need to thrive in our global society. Mr. Anthony Johnson is an educator who goes against the norm to provide his students with the necessary life skills to succeed.

Anthony Johnson is not your regular educator who followed a traditional path in life. Early on, he had to endure a myriad of hardships, which caused him to drop out of school on several occasions. For Anthony Johnson, failure was the only option he had, however, it did not deter him from pursuing a life-long dream of becoming an educator. After obtaining a GED and working hard to provide for his family financially, Mr. Johnson earned a Bachelor's degree in education. This was the impetus for the innovative educator he has become today. What makes Anthony Johnson a gem is not the fact that he is an African American male, but that he cultivates and fosters a learning environment unlike any other seen in this country.

In a highly technological society, it is imperative to note that substitution isn't innovation, it is merely the transfer of old habits using some sort of technology. Real innovation occurs when learning opportunities and experiences are modified and redefined, giving the learner an opportunity to transform the learner mindset and create new learning experiences previously inconceivable. Anthony Johnson's learning laboratory empowers young people to think about the world around them and how they can make what they learn in the classroom socially, emotionally, economically, educationally, and culturally relevant. Employing a project based learning culture is the tip of the iceberg. Mr. Johnson's students are encouraged, by extension, to enhance their zone of proximal development. Whether it is creating rap songs on the iPad using GarageBand, flying an iOS device into space, or jumping out of airplanes to illustrate the principles of velocity, Anthony Johnson's instructional practices require students to learn and think outside of the box.

As you will read in this book, you will learn about the struggles Anthony Johnson faced on his journey to success. This award-winning educator provides readers with a glimpse into #Johnsonville, a simulated real-world community that thrives in Mr. Johnson's classroom. After reading this book, you will feel empowered to take risks and transform the culture of learning in your school. Therefore, cultivating a culture of love, respect, and passion for education and learning that is relevant for all constituents within the environment.

Prologue

Many kids dream about what they want to be when they grow up.

I never did.

Some even dream of becoming a teacher.

No way. Not me. No way in hell I wanted to be a teacher.

Going all the way back to grade school, I disliked everything about schools. I hated to get on the bus every morning. After I got off the bus, I'd have to sit at a desk, bored to death with the books they made me read and stuck with boring teachers. Some of those teachers made it obvious they were only there to collect a paycheck. Right off the bat, if I didn't come off as a model student, they were as disinterested in me as I was in them. Hardly any of them made extra attempts to get me excited about their curricula.

The learning environment was neither engaging nor inviting. I'm not sure if it was because I had attention deficit hyperactivity (ADHD), attention deficit disorder (ADD) or I was just plain old *BAD*. I'm pretty sure most of my teachers thought I fit the latter category.

Admittedly, I was the teacher's worst nightmare in nearly every school I attended.

That's why it's so strange that someone like me who failed class after class wound up being a teacher.

And grab on to your seats – I love it!

It's my heart and soul.

I truly believe it was by the grace of God and His divine plan for me to choose a career as an educator. Today, that same kid who was forced to go to school practically kicking and screaming, amazingly, has been highly praised as one of the top teachers in the state of North

Carolina. I can't begin to convey how thankful I am each day to be blessed with the opportunity to share my knowledge, experience, and ability to ignite a fire under students, who like me, assumed school was the most boring place to be.

However, this learning process is not a one-way street. It's reciprocal. I am educated by every kid that I've had the opportunity to work with in the classroom as well. I learned such things as how to be a better instructor and how to construct a more productive, appealing, and interactive learning environment for them as a group as well as individually. Creating Johnsonville, a real-world simulation for my students, introduces them to software that enhances their skills and prepares them for the challenges they will ultimately encounter in life. My primary goal in working with students is that I will have a positive impact and help them in acquiring the kind of skills needed to navigate this world as they commence to choose their life's direction.

I hope that by reading my story, people will be inspired to not only tenaciously pursue their dreams, but have an awareness that sometimes the things you don't dream of might just be the perfect fit.

Chapter 1

A Troubled Beginning

I don't want my earlier comments to be misleading. As a child, I may not have dreamed about growing up to be a scientist, or a fireman, or a doctor, or a lawyer, or a teacher; but it didn't mean I was dreamless. Like many young African American males in the New Orleans neighborhood where I grew up, all the talk was about sports. I definitely wanted to play football or basketball. Yes, I envisioned being the heralded sports hero of the neighborhood who moved on to enormous riches and fame. I constantly wished to be that superstar everyone raved about as they loudly cheered while watching me on television; mesmerized by my grandiose highlight dunks or seeing me effortlessly juke panting pursuers who futilely chased me downfield to stop me from scoring my 3rd touchdown of the day.

Aside from that, I didn't really have any real direction, aspirations, or thoughts about what I wanted to do with my life. I was just kind of living in the moment, following the crowd and doing a lot of crazy stuff that I'll speak on later. Nevertheless, even though I truly loved and enjoyed playing sports. I possessed a great love for something I didn't talk about during those times - music. Man, I LOVED music. And I particularly enjoyed watching and listening to the marching bands.

Growing up in New Orleans, marching bands played a monumental role in the fabric of our culture. We have a beloved tradition of marching bands that existed prior to the birth of jazz music. I always found myself intently observing those brass marching bands during halftime of a football game or performing at funerals, street carnival celebrations, parades, and band competitions.

The dream I never took seriously was that I had this fantasy about one day becoming a band director. Simply put – I was utterly fascinated by them. Everybody in New Orleans loves a great marching band! When the marchers tromped down the street, they all takes notice! You went to the Bayou Classic to watch Southern University's spectacular performances. Nobody would dare go to the concessions stands during halftime.

What? Are you kidding me?

And miss all the excitement?

Uh, huh…it's show time!

Our football team could be down 800 – 3, but no matter what, everyone remained seat (if they weren't dancing) during halftime.

We all wanted to watch the show! The passion exhibited by the band director in charge of it all hosted a major part in my fantasy of becoming a premiere band director. Don't be fooled! I wasn't alone…many kids in New Orleans wanted to join the marching band.

But it didn't matter.

I was so doggone disgruntled with school, all it was, was just a pipe dream.

I didn't think about it at the time, but looking back, I realized my home life and surroundings weren't the most conducive environment for promoting the joys of school and earning an education. I found absolutely nothing compelling about school aside from the band. The only thing that thrilled me was hanging out with a bad crowd and learning what I could from them. It was more important to me to earn street cred then academic credentials. Frequently moving from location to location all the time and feeling like I did not have a permanent home didn't help.

Mom and dad weren't married. I think they were still together when I was born for about a year more. Actually, I have no early memories of them ever being together. I'd swing back and forth between their households; living with my mom and then my dad and grandmother. My parents resided in different neighborhoods and each contained their own set of issues.

The area where I lived with my father and grandmother was pretty rough. You had a bunch of crack addicts wandering around and people constantly on the streets dealing drugs. Yet, a block away, you'd find middle class families.

But that's how New Orleans is. One block can be completely horrible, yet, only a thousand feet away, the next block might be filled with clean cut folks and a wonderful place to grow up. The one thing I won't do is disparage New Orleans and say it was this bad place to live...it just might have not been the ideal place for me. I fell into a lot of bad associations that greatly influenced my developing persona. I ran with the wrong guys and frequently skipped school. The area I lived in provided little motivation for me to have any desire about going to college or anything else. I didn't come across many people going to college. Hardly anyone I knew ever talked about it – unless it revolved around obtaining a sports scholarship.

Most of the people I knew after high school got jobs in the area; usually in a hotel or the hospitality field. Don't get me wrong…New Orleans certainly had areas where people were more studious and motivated to attend college…just not in the vicinity I lived. Few of the people I was acquainted with graduated and then sped off to college.

My mom never went to college. She only graduated high school. Mom had 4 kids – 3 boys and 1 girl. All of us came from different daddies. Still, my mother was quite resourceful and always managed to find a way to take care of us. She worked tirelessly. Her last few years of her life, she was a transit bus driver. Sometimes she drove the route that nearest my grandmother's house. On those days, I'd spend 5 or 6 hours riding with her on the bus.

My father had two more sons I'm aware of. There were rumors of a third one, an older brother, but I never met him. My dad also finished high school. When I was young I recall him working at some type of business plant. Supposedly, he was exposed to asbestos which caused him to have many respiratory problems. Most of my life he rarely got up and worked. My great uncle owned a business, so my dad periodically would go there and work with him and paint buildings.

During my middle and high school years my father didn't have a job. He was just around. During this time, my grandmother had retired and received social security checks. My dad was on welfare and food stamps. It was pretty much our source of income. If my father wasn't at home, you could always find him hanging out at his usual spots – on corners outside of what we'd call in New Orleans bar rooms or liquor houses. It was almost guaranteed if he wasn't home he was sure to be at one of his main hangouts standing on the corner drinking alcohol.

Reflecting on my relationship with my father, I can honestly admit, he was not a good role model. I loved my father and it hurts to say this - but part of me resented him for some things, especially drinking alcohol. He'd get drunk and produce a lot of unnecessary drama. At times, thing got downright rocky in the house. I continually promised myself as a youth that when I grew up, I was not going to be this type of man. To this day, I don't drink alcohol. Those memories of my dad chugging alcohol left a huge imprint on me because I saw what it did to him and to the family. I didn't want to be that kind of father to my daughters. Having said that, despite my father's problems, when I or the family needed him – he made it a point to be there.

Early School Issues

I can trace back to when my school issues began. I attended Woodland West Elementary School in Harvey, Louisiana. Ironically, it wasn't such a bad start for me early on. I pretty much did what I was told by the teacher and scored good grades. This all changed in third grade when I moved in with my dad and grandmother. That's when my problems first began.

I attended Lincoln Elementary School, visible from my front door through the parking lot of St. Mary's Baptist Church. The start of my issues with teachers in school resulted in one of the worst ass beatings in my life. The teacher gave us homework over the weekend. Pissed off about it, I told another student, "I could kill this lady for this."

Now seriously, I didn't mean it…I was just talking trash. But guess what? That student told the teacher and she immediately called my dad. He was at the school within five minutes. He dragged my butt all the way home. I caught an whupping on the way for a block or more before I even got home for another ass whupping session. After my beating, I wanted to kick that snitch's tail and *really* kill the teacher for calling my father. I guess you could refer to that as a turning point to my school apathy. My relationship with teachers remained strained from then on. Luckily,

I passed the grade, but in the end, I wanted to get the hell out of that school. I wasn't comfortable there anymore. The other teachers knew what I had said. I felt like a target had been stamped on my back.

The next year I moved back in with my mother and returned to Woodland West. But sitting for hours listening to my teachers disinteresting lectures and doing meaningless work just wasn't doing it for me. To make matters worse in this spiritless environment, no teachers looked like me or were of the same gender. They were all women. I just couldn't relate. Plus, it was not a very inviting world to be a part of. I wasn't motivated to get any assigned work done, So, I disrupted the class and annoyed the teachers whenever I could.

Inevitably, that year I failed my studies.

During the following summer, my mom moved to another part of the Westbank of New Orleans. I started the school season at Frederick Douglass Elementary School in Gretna, Louisiana. The situation there wasn't too bad. I just hated being the oldest kid in the class. And, I was angry and irritated all the time. I can't really explain why. I turned into the prototypical school bully. I'd pick on kids just because I could get away with it. I instigated a fight with a boy much smaller than me and knocked him to the ground. Before you could blink, I leaped on top of this kid and smacked him repeatedly for no real reason at all.

Several teachers arrived and pulled me off of him. They dragged me to the school office. Nobody asked me who started the fight and why. They quickly called my mom and suspended me. For the rest of the year at Douglass, I made it my primary mission to disrupt the class so I could get sent home.

That year, they passed me on.

At some point over the summer, my family must have had a serious conversation about my behavior and made an executive decision on what steps to take for my educational future. My Aunt Carol was a high school teacher at LB Landry in

Algiers, Louisiana. After a long talk, she persuaded me to attend McDonogh #32 Elementary School, not far from her school. I moved back in with my dad and grandmother. Every teacher in that school knew my aunt. The public school was inside the city limits of New Orleans. The schools I previously attended were about 50% black and 50% white. This one was 100% African American.

The first time I ever experienced the presence of African American male teachers occurred at #32 Elementary School. I had three black male teachers in two years presiding over the class - Mr. Cole, Mr. Johnson, and Mr. Labranch. And those men didn't play; meaning they were serious about teaching and making sure you received a solid education. They left no room for error, either. You were expected to participate in class and be just as serious about getting an education, as they were to provide you with one!

The real trip is, amazingly, I flourished there!

I underwent a complete turnaround. For the first time in my life I absolutely loved going to school! My favorite teacher was Wilbert Cole. He was excellent! In fact, I thrived in his class! He kept it exciting and the class was filled with activity. There was another male teacher who taught beside him, but I forgot his name. I do remember both of them combining classes and collaborating on stuff together. It was fantastic! When I got another African American male teacher – same thing. I bloomed in his class, too! In the two fulfilling years I spent there, I missed the honor roll only once. I must say, the teachers held up their end and I held up mine.

Unfortunately for me, McDonogh #32 was only a K-6 school.

Chapter 2

The Struggle

When I reflect back on those early school years it's still astounding that I attended 8 different schools in 10 years. Most people would assume that after finally achieving academic success those last couple of years it would have been a notable turning point for me.

That's what you'd assume.

Except that was far from the case. I reverted back to boredom with school and hating it.

I had a choice of staying in Algiers and attending Berman Jr. High or returning to Marrero and enrolling in Ellender Middle.

No real decision.

I chose Ellender because I wanted to play football there.

Turned out to be a big mistake.

In retrospect, I should have stayed in Algiers. Once again, I ended up a teacher's nightmare. I couldn't stay out of trouble. And didn't really want to. I remember throwing a trashcan across the classroom one day and was immediately sent to the principal's office. I presumed I'd be suspended, but got something else instead. The assistant principal (AP) owned a paddle and smacked me so many times the leftover marks looked like I'd been branded! I furiously warned him that when I got home I was going to tell my dad. No teacher had the right to do that to me! My father would take care of it.

The threat backfired. The AP challenged my belligerence and made me call my father.

Dad wasn't happy…

with ME!

Instead, the AP received the green light from my father to do whatever is necessary to discipline me. And so, paddling at school and whippings at home resumed for the rest of the year. Still, it didn't change my behavior. It just built up more animosity between the teachers and me. I failed my classes and continued to get into trouble due to all the fights I got involved in.

Halfway through the school year, the only choice I was given was to move back in with my mother. Plus, I could only go to Gretna Jr. High because she lived in that area. All of this was against my wishes. I hated the school, the football team, and the school colors.

Before long my foolishness got me suspended again. In one incident, I swaggered out of class. My sole mission had been to disrupt the class and do everything possible to get suspended. It worked – I got myself suspended twice. I really didn't want to be at that school. Moreover, I didn't have any friends at Gretna. I knew if I made a name for myself and did something really bad and unruly they would be forced to send me back to the middle school I wanted to be in.

My stint with the school lasted three weeks.

I got what I wanted. I was happy to go back to Ellender and recommence my disorderly conduct. I failed the 7th grade. And when I finally got into the 8th grade I failed it too. The school administration surrendered to my uncooperative behavior. They offered me the option of attending summer school for one of the classes I failed so I could advance to high school. I took them up on it and went to summer school. I barely did any worthwhile work, but still passed.

When I reflect on those years, I think about what kind of crap went on to allow a failing student to pass through school without a proper education. Was it laziness? A need to fill a quota? Apathy? Teacher burnout?

All of it?

Sure, it was great for me at the time, but totally unfair to hard working students who deserved it. I couldn't fathom what compelled an instructor who should be dedicated to their craft to give a recognizably undeserving student a pass. It's akin to handing a driver's license to a person who has never started a car and then letting them drive freely on the streets and highways.

You cannot allow that person to drive. He or she is an obvious danger to all fellow drivers and pedestrians. Consequently, no one should ever be given an easy ride through the educational system if they fail to fulfill the class requirements.

What's appalling to me today is that educators are still inexcusably giving away passes or good scores to students who truly don't deserve it. It's so ridiculously unfair to those who have worked their butts off to get a passing grade or score an "A" in class. Yet these instructors don't seem to understand or care, that they are perpetrating an injustice and by doing so, causing kids more harm than good.

Look, I can certainly relate to empathizing with a child who may come from circumstances of poverty, whereas life has not been kind to them; but that still doesn't justify handing them a grade they don't deserve simply because. Feeling sorry for them doesn't prepare or provide them with the necessary technical and coping skills they will need to maneuver their way through life's obstacles.

Another thing I observed during the early years of my journey through the educational system is that none of the teachers I experienced took the time aside to converse with me privately and find out what was going on inside me and what caused me to be so combative. I don't remember a single teacher during that time attempting to encourage or inspire me.

I attended John Ehret High School in Marrero, Louisiana for about a year and a half. At Ehret I indulged in my favorite pastime – playing around. The only thing that held ANY interest for me in school was the third period band and after-school band practice. The other classes I could care less about. Half of them I snubbed and didn't bother to attend.

One day, in my second year in the ninth grade they asked me to come into the counselor's (office around 9:00 AM. I wondered, why I was being called in so early in the morning? I hadn't done anything yet! When I walked in, I found my dad sitting there waiting for me.

The school counselor had phoned my father and told him that my being there was a complete waste of everyone's time…including my own. Basically, I was being kicked out of school. The counselor moved on to say that since I was no longer a part of their high school program I should consider signing up for a General Education Development (GED) program. Then I could work on earning a high school equivalency credential and afterwards learn a trade.

That woke me up!

All of a sudden school took on a new appeal. I pleaded my case and begged to stay. I promised to change my attitude, behavior, whatever it took if they'd just let me stay. But it was too late. The decision had been made. It was over. I was handed a form and instructed to present it to each of my teachers so they could sign off on it. Out of all the teachers, only one asked me to reconsider. That was Mrs. Green. The rest of them may not have outwardly smiled, but the expression on their faces informed me they were greatly relieved.

And ecstatic to finally get me the hell out of their faces!

It's a day I will never forget.

My folks tried to tell me…especially my mother. She constantly warned me about what would happen if I didn't get it together in school soon.

But I didn't listen.

My mother used to tell me to act right, but it was like she spoke to a wall. My grandmother used to get on me all the time regarding the same thing. Conversely, I had family members, not in my household, who proved to be successful. My aunt was an excellent educator and some of my cousins were also teachers. That's why I ended up at McDonogh #32 Elementary School whereby I achieved so much early success. My aunt taught high school only about a half mile away from McDonogh's. That's another reason I started acting right in that school apart from the wonderful teachers. If I got in trouble I could expect she'd get a call.

All those times I talked trash and daydreamed about walking out of school forever finally became a reality. I got my ill-conceived wish. I may have tried to fool myself, but honestly, I was depressed. Despite the counselor's advice, I felt lost and unsure. I had no idea what life now had in store for me.

Chapter 3

A Working Man

So, time passed, and it was January of 1989.
My K-12 career was concluded without any
fanfare. No high school graduation ceremony.
No walking on stage with my robes flowing to
accept my high school degree. No tossing my
graduation cap in the air and cherishing that

moment of unity with my fellow graduates as we all heave a sigh of relief and joy that we finally graduated from high school. I couldn't participate in any discussions about what are you going to do after graduation? What college are you going to? There were no grad night celebrations. No looking forward to our 10-year high school reunion so we could look back on our crazy high school memories.

Nope. That was not my story.

The majority of people I attended high school with reminisce fondly about their high school years, others maybe not so much. It's possible they didn't have a great experience…but nevertheless, unlike me, they still graduated.

Sure, I could offer you all kinds of excuses and cite numerous reasons as to why school didn't work out for me – ranging from my distracting home environment to being saddled with horrible instructors – and, to a certain extent - I would be right! Some of those factors, without question, contributed to making my schooling difficult. But after all was said and done, it didn't matter one damn bit. The end result still fell upon my shoulders.

No high school degree.

No certificates.

No class awards.

It was my fault and my burden. Ultimately, I really didn't have anyone to blame but myself. I had no choice but to take responsibility for my mistakes and own up to the consequences of my actions. No one held Anthony Johnson at gunpoint and forced him to ditch classes. Anthony Johnson did that all by his lonesome. Anthony Johnson is the one that instigated most of the fights he got into. Anthony Johnson is the one that caused the teachers' unending grief.

Nevertheless, what's done is done. I couldn't magically turn the clock back and start over. Groundhog's day was just a fable, a movie. I couldn't relive the past over and over again until I got it right. Now it was up to me to make something happen, otherwise, I'd end up standing on the same corner as my father every day sipping from a paper bag that disguised my alcoholic beverage. All of a sudden, I had been thrust into a cold unrelenting world that didn't give a shit about my plight. I was just another high school dropout statistic among millions of others in the same circumstance. I felt like I had been unceremoniously shot from a canon:

BOOM!

Welcome to the world of adults, Anthony Johnson!

My last option was to sit down and do some hard thinking about what I planned to do with the rest of my life. One thing loomed over my head like a cloud – I eventually received my G.E.D. - but I HAD NO SKILLS.

I possessed nothing of value that I could readily and proudly show displaying my qualifications for a desired job position. I hadn't developed any relationships with teachers or mentors or anyone willing to write an outstanding letter of recommendation for me that I could proudly hand to a potential employer.

Man, I needed to get my stuff together and I needed to do so fast! At this stage, the only person I could truly depend on was me.

I thought about all the things that went wrong for me in school and why I ended up in this debilitating predicament. As I delved into my mindset about how I handled my past school years, I realized that I tended to live in the moment, giving little thought about how my ugly daily behavior would shape my tomorrows. Most of the people around me were exactly the same way.

But I couldn't use that as an excuse. I still made the choice to do the things I did.

The craziest thing about it is, it's not like I didn't know the scholastic material presented to me – because I did! Yes, it was often challenging…but I rarely gave myself credit for how intelligent I really was. I learned in later years that this is not that unusual with a lot of young men, especially those involved in athletics or raised in rough environments. We often disguise how naturally bright we are because it makes us look weak to others. Acting like a nerd by being studious and knowing the answers to questions posed by the teachers doesn't signify being tough. Speaking "proper" English is not "cool. For young African American males, particularly, it means we're acting "white" or trying to appear more sophisticated and better than anyone else. We're told "Get real" "Don't be acting all fake!" "Keep it 100%."

But most of all, we fear being laughed at and mocked repeatedly by our peers.

Another reason I didn't perform well in my classes is because I found them BORING! It's as simple as that. If not, WHY is it that for the two years I spent at McDonogh #32 Elementary School, I excelled working with very difficult material? The answer is, the teachers in that school got me excited and motivated about learning! I can't emphasize that enough! As I mentioned earlier, I no longer dreaded going to school –- I LOVED going to school during those too brief years. Once I changed schools, boredom overtook me again.

That's why I acted out. I'm sure I could have done significantly better in those classes if I had the same type of teachers that were as passionate about teaching as the ones at McDonogh. Returning to the monotony of sitting at that desk for hours reading dull material and trying to listen to unimaginative instructors just didn't work for me.

Nonetheless, in order for me to move forward I'd have to discover a way to override those barriers that I allowed to affect my progress for so many years. My New Year's resolution was to take control of my life

In the fall of 1989, I enrolled in Southern University at New Orleans (SUNO) with the expressed purpose of majoring in Computer Science. By the end of the semester my GPA had sunk to a miserable 0.50.

And just like that, my higher education excursion was over and done with.

College was worse in my opinion than high school. Of course, once again, it fell on me. I had spent the vast amount of my time hanging out at the student union. I found it much more engaging than the classroom. A year after flunking out of SUNO, surprisingly, I found a job that didn't require major academic skills and it paid pretty good wages.

It didn't take long for me to find out why I got the job so easily. It was hard ass work that required a special kind of skill – survival! Not many people stayed on this job very long because it's not exactly what I would consider a "safe" environment. I worked as a correctional officer in the Orleans Parish Sheriff's office (OSPO) supervising the inmates in its correctional facility.

I applied one week and within a week they assigned me to work jail duty. It was absolutely insane with all kinds of crazy stuff going on. What made absolutely no sense to me on the day I started working at the Orleans Parish system, is that the new employees were given khaki uniforms instead of the black ones worn by the regular deputies. You must wear these khaki uniforms for a 3-month probationary period. I couldn't stand it! It was like having a bullseye target tattoocd on your back. It signals to the inmates that you are new. They are not going to listen to anything you have to say. Everything you try to do is challenged by the inmates until you hopefully gain their respect. The day I began working in the jail I immediately got into fist fights. Routinely, there was always someone trying to test me.

We worked 12 hour shifts, four days on and four days off. Each shift I was required to go into the dorm of 44 inmates by myself carrying a clipboard. The inmates were ordered to stand at the back of the room and await roll call. Once I called their name they'd walk past and show me their arm band. After that, they'd stand on the other side of the room. Keep in mind, there's a reason these guys are in jail – they don't follow the law! So, picture me, a 19-year-old deputy, wearing a khaki uniform. It was my duty to go in and instruct them on what to do. First of all, they don't feel like getting up at 6:00 AM. Secondly, they've got me waking them up and telling them what needs to be done. Consequently, every morning, 4 days a week, I had to endure being cussed out and/or fighting with an inmate.

Once roll call was completed, inmates came out of the dorm, got their breakfast, and headed back in. To keep them in check, one deputy would stand out and we'd count 5 individuals, let them come in, and then go back and get 5 more. Well, I was the deputy counting one day and I put my hand up. An inmate smacked my hand and belligerently strolled out. When I grabbed him by the back of the shirt and pulled him into the dorm he turned around and hit me. Now we're throwing down.

After 90 days, I was finally able to switch to a black uniform. I managed to stay at that job for about 9 or 10 months before I quit. The primary reason I left the job is because I viewed the system as corrupt. One day I was going in to do my roll call when one of the inmates pulled me aside and whispered: "Johnson, don't go in there." He informed me that a deputy had given one of the inmates a knife and intended to hold me hostage. I discovered later that this particular deputy got arrested. He used to covertly give the inmates things like wavy grease, hair brushes, doo rags, and more that. The inmates asked him for a knife and he had to give it to them, otherwise, they'd expose him for all the contraband he slipped into the jail. How in the hell could I work any longer in a dangerous environment with fellow deputies that I didn't trust?

Afterwards, I bounced around from job to job for a couple of years, living from paycheck to paycheck, and robbing Peter to pay Paul. In April of 1994, I attained a job at the Jefferson Parish

Sheriff's Office outside of New Orleans. I worked 8-hour shifts and enjoyed working there much more than at the OSPO jail system. It also paid more. My finances improved, but unfortunately not enough to prevent my car from being repossessed. On top of it all, I was forced to file a Chapter 11 bankruptcy. It was the most humiliating period of my life. Truthfully, those words don't even begin to describe a fraction of how deeply ravaged my emotions were.

At the time, I started viewing life differently. I resolved in my mind, I must be here for a purpose. It took me awhile before I recognized that the truth had been staring me in the face. No matter how much I whined about my life, it could have been worse. Ironically, some of the guys I went to school with at Ehret were inmates in the correctional facility I worked in. The same dudes I often skipped school with were now under my control as a correctional officer. I prayed to God and thanked Him for keeping me from ever serving time behind bars. I counted my blessings daily that I was granted the freedom to go home each day after suffering through eight hours in that hell hole. I could have easily been one of those guys incarcerated.

Still, regrets about my actions in school began emerging again. I'd replay them often and they'd swirled through my head like a blender. I decided to take another shot at school again. I promptly enrolled at Delgado Community College in New Orleans. This was after finally moving past all my denials. I admitted to myself how much I wished I had behaved in class, graduated from high school, and attended Southern University to march in their bands.

I guess you could say that although I may not have had dreams or aspirations as a child, I was certainly having them as a young adult.

When I finally reached the point that I was sincerely ready to educate myself and pursue a degree from college, I simultaneously faced a brutal truth I was forced to stop ignoring:

Anthony Johnson was deficient in the necessary skills he needed to succeed in whatever career chose to go after.

It hurt for me to acknowledge my academic inadequacies. Those deficiencies included not knowing how to write in complete sentences and struggling with basic math; things I should have learned years ago. Swallowing my pride, I enrolled in remedial courses and battled through my shortcomings.

I believe that this was the first time I genuinely became responsible and accepted accountability for all my past school discretions. That new and powerful drive bolstered me and helped to propel me over those mental hurdles that kept insistently obstructing my vision.

Chapter 4

A Move and A New Direction

People thought I had lost my mind for leaving one of the best jobs I ever had at the Jefferson-Parish Sheriff's department. I was repeatedly asked, "Why are you leaving a job like that after it took you a couple of years to get on with them?"

I understood the question. I probably would have asked the same thing if I saw someone else in a similar position leave such a great job. I was aware it was a gamble, but it was something I needed to do. No matter what, I will always be grateful for the job at the Sheriff's department because that's when I met my wife, Dr. Desiree Johnson. We met each other one night on New Year's Eve and all I can say is – from that moment on, you could call it a "wrap." We've been together ever since.

Desiree and I were complete opposites. She graduated near the top of her class and loved school. When we starting dating, she was in a last year of medical school. She graduated from Wellesley College. I admit I was a little intimated by her success and level of education. I kept my own skeletons in the closet until after she fell in love. When I opened up to her about past, she embraced and encouraged me to move forward. We've been together ever since.

Just when it seemed life things were turning around for the better, on June 27, 1998, one of the most cataclysmic events in my life happened. No matter how much you think you are emotionally prepared for the inevitable death of someone you dearly love, who has been suffering, you never really are. On that day, we buried my mom in New Orleans. She died from breast cancer a week earlier. There was hardly any time for me to absorb it all. The very next day we moved to

Salisbury, North Carolina, where my wife had planned to establish her practice.

Desiree and I had formulated multiple plans together and joyfully looked forward to how great it would be to move and start a whole new life with our newly born first child. It should have been an invigorating time for me…

But instead, I was steeped in depression.

Nothing in the world can prepare you for kissing your cold mom one last time before they close her casket. Even though I had the company of my beautiful wife and daughter, I felt very alone. At this dark moment in time I hated living in North Carolina where I didn't know a soul…and I hated life. But no matter how terrible

I was feeling, I needed to dig down deeper within myself. There happened to be this little person in our household who depended on us and required our attention. Her world should be enriched with all the beauty life offered, not the pitfalls.

The cliché rings true: "Life Goes On."

My wife and I agreed I'd be a stay-at-home dad for a year. Staying at home would provide a chance for me to get my act together. I would have the time to search for a trustworthy person to babysit our daughter. Within a month of moving here, Dr. Catrelia Steele Hunter (at the time an administrator at Livingstone College and later its Acting President) invited us to Trinity Presbyterian Church where her husband was pastor.

The very first person we met in church was Mrs. Annie Bates. At first when we walked in, I tried to make a move to sit in the back of the church. But Mrs. Bates wasn't having it. She escorted us to the middle of the sanctuary and immediately struck up a conversation. It was exactly what was prescribed...that warm feeling of friendship. I didn't know her, but after we talked, I felt like we'd been friends for years.

The church greatly comforted me and assisted me in dealing with the troubling issues I was confronted with at the time. I became quick friends with her sons, Pastor Timothy Bates and George Bates III. The Bates family and members of Trinity made Salisbury feel like home. Life in Salisbury, North Carolina was starting to feel pretty good after all. I met a lot of downhome folks and enjoyed the camaraderie.

In December, Desiree and I were very excited about our first Christmas in our new home. I recall us standing there admiring our tree filled with decorations when I received a call from New Orleans to go down and check on my dad. I assumed things would be fine. He had been in the hospital plenty of times before. It was no big deal…or so I thought. I figured he would spend a couple of days at the hospital and, as usual, be released to return home. During my flight back to North Carolina, he passed away. I didn't know it at the time.

When I got home I instantly sensed something was wrong the moment I stepped inside the door. My wife broke the news to me. Once again, my world imploded. I collapsed back into that bottomless chasm of despondency. Emotionally I was a major wreck; so much so my thoughts became distorted. In hindsight, I find it hard to believe I sank to such a low… I actually began hating anyone who spoke about both of their parents being alive. I didn't want to be anywhere around them. I struggled mightily to combat these absurd feelings that were spiraling out of control. I did not want to be that person. Logically I was aware such thoughts were ridiculous. But upon deeper meditation, I realized that Anthony Johnson had reached the height of selfishness.

What Anthony Johnson needed to be was selfless.

The holidays had arrived. It was my daughter Jessieca's first Christmas. No matter how difficult it was, I labored to cast those negative emotions aside. It was paramount I focused on making sure the holidays were fun for Jessieca. I had to keep reminding myself – it's not about you! Fortunately, I somehow managed to compartmentalize my feelings, but it was a major strain. The loss of my folks within such a short span of time was devastating. I loved my parents so much and it hurt to no longer have them play a role in my life. So many times, I wanted to pick up the phone and talk to them on that special day and joyfully share the news about our new family's first Christmas.

I missed them terribly.

I have always considered myself a strong man...fearless...someone who fought some hardcore dudes in my time; especially when I worked the jail system. Now I felt immobilized, helpless, and fighting a battle that was impossible to win. Losing my parents in 1998 within six months of each other was the most brutal and longest stretch in my existence.

I engaged in a tremendous amount of soul searching during this period. Once more I was beset by those unwanted demons that constantly appeared to invade my world; leaving me with nothing but the detritus to pick up from my own missteps. I spent endless hours pondering concerns and questions about my life's direction.

Why does this shit always happen to me?

Where did I go wrong?

What does God have in store for me?

Is it too late?

While everyone else looked forward to the New Year so they could finally join in Prince's musical quest to get down and "Party like it's 1999," instead, all I thought about was what would 1999 and the new millennium bring into my life.

It was a time of meditation. I mentally time-travelled back to my elementary years to seek out the reasons. Fourth grade is where I pinpointed my life's serious downturn, setting the course that lead to my current state of misery. I prayed over and over again for God to please show me how to take control of my life and turn it all around.

I got my answer.

In the fall of 1999, I enrolled in Livingstone College as a music major, the only subject I ever had a remote interest in. I was thrilled about my decision. My mindset was to make a difference musically and produce some avant-garde stuff. The very first day of registration, I was informed that I needed to sign up for the marching band. I didn't realize Livingstone College had a marching band until registration. As I mentioned, I loved marching bands, especially, the Southern

University Marching Band. Yet, I politely declined to do so. I was immediately told that it was a requirement of the music program.

The advisor sent me to the band director's office to outline my reasons for not wanting to participate in the marching band. I explained to the band director, Dr. Gary Callahan, my discomfort in joining the marching band. I was a twenty-eight-year-old freshman with a wife and a kid. I maintained I would feel out of place at my age and didn't have the time nor energy to march with a bunch of teenagers.

Dr. Callahan conferred that he understood the concern about my age, but it was mandatory for music majors to march in the band. We debated the whole thing for nearly forty-five minutes until he finally grew tired of it and gave me an ultimatum – march or find another major. It pissed me off. I didn't like anyone giving me ANY kind of ultimatum or pushing my back up against the wall…but I also remembered how much success I had walking out of past school programs…

This time I didn't retreat…I stepped forward.

I joined the Livingstone College marching band.

I'm very proud to say I am now a self-proclaimed band head. Livingstone College played a substantial part in helping me to find myself and my purpose. I had professors who pushed and motivated me in ways I needed. But the difference this time is, I didn't shove back or rebel against it…I thirsted for it. I was determined to excel, a desire that escaped me in my earlier years. During my undergraduate days, I even pledged to the Kappa Alpha Psi Fraternity and joined a brotherhood of like-minded men. My Frat brothers pushed me well beyond what I considered my limitations. Better yet, I learned the only limitations to my success were the obstacles I dropped in front of me.

During my freshman year at Livingstone I volunteered at Isenberg Elementary School to fulfill my college community service requirements. At once, I noticed little had changed since the last time I attended elementary school so many years ago. The lessons were not engaging and failed to encourage collaboration or critical thinking. Students were still given worksheets for at least half of the time they were in school.

The teacher sat chained to her desk and made no effort to walk throughout the classroom and connect with her students. She barely paid any personal attention to the students apart from teaching the lessons. When I started volunteering, it was like she couldn't wait to get up and leave as soon as I entered the classroom. She would leave me alone in the class with the students for hours. She made no real effort to communicate with me either. I had no idea where she'd go or what she did when she vanished. I was so disturbed by what I observed of her apathy in the classroom I tried to take a more active role as a volunteer and mentor so the students would get at least something out of it.

One thing that really upset me was when I caught a student sleeping in the back of the classroom. I pointed him out to the teacher. Her exact response was, "Let him sleep." She claimed it was better that this student, who often misbehaved, remain asleep so she could more efficiently manage the class. I couldn't believe what I heard. I guess it angered me more than it might someone else. I saw myself in that kid. I could project the pain and struggle in store for him in the future. I wondered if he'd have the wherewithal to one day self-reflect and analyze like I did, what point in his life he took that bad swing.

I wanted so badly to grab him, shake him, and yell:

Dude, WAKE THE HELL UP! Don't you see what's going on? They're allowing you to sleep away your potential to someday be a successful person! Man, don't let them do this to you! And don't do it to yourself! Trust me. I know. I've been where you're at, and it's a NOWHERE STREET! Nobody talked to me either and when they did, I ignored them because it wasn't often enough. I either slept, disrupted the class, picked a fight, or walked out of the classroom. I'm here to tell you – it did me no good! Sometimes they even insultingly gave me a passing grade just to get me out of their faces. I had the false illusion that I did okay in class, but it came back to haunt me. One day you'll open your eyes and really become WOKE. On that day, you'll sadly realize you-don't-know-crap! So, don't wait until you're an adult and suddenly find out the doors of opportunity are bolt locked because you weren't properly educated. I know who you are…you are me. Don't go through what I dealt with - start the process NOW while you're still young!

I didn't say it to him, but I've said it to a lot of students since that time. I've devoted my life to making sure students I encounter, especially those similar to me as a youth, know where I stand.

It may seem like such a minor incident...even the smartest kids sometimes nod off in class...but for me it triggered an alarm that screamed loudly in my head. It's like he might not have awakened, but I sure in the hell did! I found my purpose in life watching that youngster sound asleep in the back of that class while the other students completed their worksheets. What I observed about this teacher, which could be applied to many teachers today, is that their way of resolving problems with students with behavior issues is to let them sleep in class or completely remove them from the classroom environment so they can operate the classroom more efficiently. Sadly, the student ends up being the sacrificial lamb so that others can improve and become better.

That night I went home and shared this experience with my wife. I was Mr. Motor-mouth and couldn't stop talking about it! I told her I'd been seriously thinking about changing my major and sought her opinion about the matter. The truth is, I had already resolved to change my major to elementary education. Thankfully, Desiree, being the person she is, found it a wonderful idea for me to revise my goals and offered nothing but her complete support.

The next semester, I changed my major to elementary education. I received a full academic scholarship, which seemed to further validate my new career path. The school system was in the midst of heavily recruiting African-American male teachers. Any student who signed a contract to stay and teach in the school district would receive a full scholarship. I didn't hesitate to sign. At long last God helped me to find my calling.

In my education classes, I shared my experience in school with my professors. I talked about how I was going to make it my mission to find ways to get students excited about school and how it would entail a different approach to teaching. I discussed how my schoolroom would not be just a class but a learning space.

I got blindsided by the response.

Several professors told me that I would be unemployed by the end of the first school year and that my idealistic approach to education was all wrong. These educators psychoanalyzed me as this angry and bitter person who was determined NOT to make a real difference in my student's lives as I declared, but rather, I was on a crusade to prove that teachers were the ones at fault for failing schools. They said I had been nursing an age-old grudge and remained furious for years because of my clashes with teachers.

As much as it infuriated me, I had to also admit there may be some truth to what they preached. After volunteering and working as a mentor in some very good classrooms with excellent and dedicated teachers, my view eventually changed. I found a compromise between my anger and frustration with the bad teachers I experienced and the outstanding educators devoted to their craft who made every effort to improve the lives of their students. Moreover, I had to acknowledge the rage and indifference within me that blocked my willingness to learn during my youth. All of those attributes served me well in the forthcoming years because my education wasn't going to be solely derived from educators – it would come from paying heed to my students, as well.

In 2003, I graduated with a bachelor's degree in Elementary Education. I suspected there was a shortage, but I didn't know at the time there was only ONE African American male school elementary school teacher in my entire district when I was going to college!

Nevertheless, I was ready. I couldn't wait to jump out there and pursue my goal to make a difference.

Chapter 5

Johnsonville: The Collaborative Learning Community

It's still hard for me to believe that the niche
I wound up carving out for myself was to be a
teacher. I can imagine some of my peers from
elementary and high school shaking their heads
and saying repeatedly: "No way! Anthony? Him?

A teacher? C'mon now, stop lying to me! Okay, so seriously...what really happened to him?"

What happened is I am currently living an extraordinary life as a teacher. And I wouldn't have it any other way. This has turned out to be an ideal career for me. The learning never ends and I sincerely enjoy it! I'm also pleased because I stayed true to myself and took on the challenge each and every day to work on keeping my students excited about the subjects we explore and the overall educational process.

My focus as a teacher is to provide my students learning experiences radically different from my own. I continually strive to create informative, yet fun projects, and a classroom atmosphere that shows students the benefits of an education. I don't want them to be bored or fearful of learning something new. I take great pride in developing a child's innate desire to learn, especially ones who live in environments that place little value on the attributes of receiving an education.

I want to scream with joy (sometimes I do!) when I work with a student who enters my classroom hating school but leaves eager to find out what project I have in store for them the next day. I do my best to encourage kids that have had bad experiences in prior classrooms to discard their fears and negative attitudes and trust that this experience will be one that they'll enjoy. It is indescribable to explain just how good I feel when I see a student whose face was formerly devoid of expression beaming with excitement due to successfully implementing objectives designed for the class.

My classroom, better known as Johnsonville, isn't a typical classroom at all. It's a collaborative community – a real-world simulation of adulthood whereby kids come to work and plan while they learn about personal finance, government, and global affairs. I integrate technology and problem-based learning (PBL) to capture the attention of even the most disengaged students.

Think about this. The general purpose of schools is to educate and prepare students for the jobs and occupations available in today's economy once they graduate.

Are employees evaluated using bubble-in tests to prove they know the ins and outs of their job?

Do they learn and use new skills one at a time in a vacuum?

The questions may sound a bit silly until you realize too often that's what students take away from their education. Why is there a culture to drill facts into students heads just to pass a test?

Let's get real.

The reality of standardized exams is that you are not awarded points based upon what you know. You are given points based on what answers you select and bubble-in on your answer sheet. Your score depends on how well or poorly you fill in those bubbles. A high score means you've achieved success – on paper. But that doesn't necessarily mean that type of success will transfer into the real world. Success in any endeavor depends on how well you execute and excel at both the small and large tasks a job demands. Employees in today's economy aren't evaluated using formal assessments to prove they know the ins and outs of their job. They're assessed based on their overall performance. I can't stress that enough – "overall performance!" That two-word phrase lies at the heart of my student evaluations.

Notwithstanding, that doesn't mean I don't emphasize the importance of students earning the highest grades they can in their school career…I just want them to represent the complete package when they move on from my tutelage. I hope to see them utilize to the best of their ability the knowledge gained in Johnsonville as they navigate through the obstacles they are sure to encounter in the real world.

This was a major part of my thinking when I dove into designing the Johnsonville program. Just like in the real world, my students demonstrate what they can do through projects, teamwork, and research. I've never been a big believer in teaching students how to pass a test. Indeed, since my first year in the classroom, I've used a project-based learning model with my science and social studies classes.

Here's how it works.

On the first day of school, I issued my fifth graders a PASSPORT (Preparing All Students for Success by Participating in an Ongoing Real-World simulation using Technology). This was followed by my explanation that their yearlong adventure to "Johnsonville" starts today. The school year constitutes a simulation of adulthood where students work, create, and learn about personal finances and entrepreneurial skills. The students experience real-world situations and gain insights into global affairs. The program model enables students to view my class less as a traditional "classroom" and more as an interactive city where all projects intertwine to create an ecosystem encompassing businesses and homes.

During the first week of the school program, my students are instructed to write a classroom constitution. The constitution gives them a voice and ownership in the classroom. Before my district went one to one with iPads, I ceremoniously issued each student $1,000 in Johnsonville cash so they could get their working lives started in the simulation. I learned by trial and error that this was not a good practice to undertake. Students were constantly stealing money from each other. Presently, all monetary transactions are online using iPads.

Once the constitution and orientation part of the program is completed it becomes time to start assigning seating and rent for a particular location. For example, the futons are designated as the premium seats and feature a cost of $2,000 a week. The bar costs $1,500 per week and the tables $500. Next, to make the simulation come alive, I would print 3D models to create a model city of Johnsonville. If a 3D printer was not available, the alternative was to employ paper models or shoeboxes. When I created Johnsonville out of college, I used shoe boxes for houses and shipping boxes for skyscrapers. Over the years, I upgraded from paper models to 3D models. Supplying a physical representation of the city entices the students to be motivated about participating.

All participants have a job in the beginning of the simulation. One of the most fun things for students to create during the first couple of days of school is the business cards. Each student must create a card with "Student" as their occupation. Student jobs pay $100 per day. Later in the school year, each student has the opportunity to become an entrepreneur, a politician, or a banker. Students are required to pay for a house or rent an apartment, earn wages, and manage their finances.

As the children buy and sell items I donate, the advantage of this system, is that they learn career-oriented math skills coupled with life lessons. Just like they would in a real business, they manage a database of their clients or suppliers, create advertising plans, and track their income to ensure they are making a profit.

I incorporated politics in Johnsonville, which is a particularly relevant subject in these troubled times. Students are taught the different levels and branches of government and hold elections for positions of power, including president and city council. Furthermore, ambitious students can earn extra money through academic achievements and good behavior.

For those of you in the teaching profession who are interested in creating an environment like Johnsonville in your classroom, the first thing I advise you to do is to stop thinking of yourself solely as a teacher and visualize yourself more as a classroom facilitator. PBL through its real-world simulation is all about educators yielding control of their classrooms to students and allowing them the chance to take charge of their learning and explore answers for themselves.

Step two is to build lessons and experiences that you feel are relevant to your students. Present them with real-world issues such as buying a home, paying rent, starting a business, and managing finances. The PBL model equips students to confront many of the same situations that adults encounter. They can equate what happens in the classroom to what's going on in the real-world.

The relevance of this is that it makes each lesson more memorable. Students are more likely to remember the overall concept of an experience as opposed to memorizing facts for a test; facts that often disappear as soon as the kid steps outside the classroom.

I've been granted the opportunity of seeing firsthand the favorable results of my work with students. Not enough students get the chance to be taught by a male teacher because there are still so few in a field dominated by female educators.

Even so, I am pleased to report that engaging students with the PBL model had produced a positive impact on my students. I'd like to elaborate a little further on this. My accountability measures focus on the whole child and are based on real-world approaches. In my classrooms, my students are immediately made aware of what is expected of them, along with the understanding that I have high expectations in regard to their performance. And you know what? They willingly give 110 percent of themselves as they strive for excellence.

In a learning environment where the norm is flying drones, launching weather balloons into space and utilizing technology to expand their zone of proximal development, my students recognize they are accountable for whatever they learn. Whether it is accountable talk stems, Webb's depth of knowledge, or think-pair-share experiences, my students always self-assess and hold themselves responsible for their edification. One thing to keep in mind, is that we are preparing students for a global economy and jobs that may not exist! We need to reevaluate the experiences we give our students and a more comprehensive measurement of the growth they show at the end of each school year. They should not be judged by just one End-of-Grade Test.

There are many critical issues in public education right now such as standardized testing, low pay for teachers, student engagement, and classroom size to name only a few. At this point I emphatically maintain that too many classrooms in our public schools' lack student engagement primarily due to a gap between students and educators.

According to a fellow TED-ED Innovative Educator, Kristin Long, who has a project entitled Roll Call, over 80 percent of public school students are kids of color. Moreover, almost 80 percent of public school teachers are female; yet approximately half of our students are male.

Religion?

Household income?

Music preference?

All of these gaps have influenced the classroom. I sincerely believe we can close these gaps with PBL and the method of using real-world simulation. My experiences as a student are unique when compared to the majority of my fellow educators. Student engagement is crucial to me. Although I've been rewarded with a long list of accolades behind my name, it's a shared experience. My students have taught me everything I know and have guided me to where I am today.

I'm truly blessed to have achieved such incredible success in my fifth-grade science and social studies classroom at Isenberg Elementary. I've been bestowed with a multitude of honors and accolades as a teacher including cash stipends and a one-year lease on a vehicle from Gerry Wood Honda. Another cherished award was being named the "2016 Teacher of the Year." It left me shocked, speechless, and feeling like the world had suddenly become surreal; especially when Superintendent Dr. Lynn Moody remarked, "Anthony Johnson breaks the mold."

My mission as an educator has always been to be innovative, keep updated and aware of the ever-changing technology, and to do what I can to positively influence and leave my imprint on shaping education to conform and embrace all student's needs. That's why I doggedly promote the PBL concept and model, as applied to student learning - because it WORKS! I believe in its educational effectiveness and proven benefits; but even more importantly – so do my students – and their parents, too, who have been very supportive! Throughout my travels here and abroad, I have unabashedly declared that one of the best solutions to increasing student engagement is by implementing PBL into the school system.

We must keep in mind that every child is unique and has a different learning capacity.

Relating classroom lessons to real life helps students at any level to connect with the content and interpret it in a way they can understand. When students become part of their learning process they take pride in the education and become more engaged. PBL not only keeps students busy, but it allows each one to show what they've learned in a creative, supportive, and collaborative environment. Recently, I have installed robotics and a maker space in the classroom. My students have also been involved in working on projects publishing their own books and/or creating music videos. In addition, they have learned how to use technology to read, play music, or just have fun!

Designing a classroom to promote essential 21st-century skills that students need to thrive and compete in today's job market is critical to student engagement and just as vitally important – a positive self-image. The PBL system will not cast away the student who does not perform well on standardized exams like driftwood. Instead, PBL chooses to embrace that student and help ready them for pursuit of a career in the real-world.

Chapter 6

Creating Your Own "Johnsonville"

To reiterate: in Johnsonville, students explore issues such as buying a home, paying rent, paying mortgage and taxes, starting a business, and managing finances. Students see adults face these same problems and make the connection from what happens in Johnsonville to the real world. Relevance makes each lesson memorable; meaning students are more likely to remember the overall concept of an experience as opposed to memorizing facts for a test. It's evident my past has guided my impetus to push students to deal with reality, not theory.

If you are a teacher and interested in integrating PBL into your curriculum, here's some suggestions below and in the following chapters on how you can make PBL relevant to your students.

Encourage Collaboration

In a conventional schoolroom, desks are designed for individual students – which is why I don't have any. In my classroom, you will only find tables, collaboration bars, and sofas that provide a certain type of ambience and offer the perfect furnishings for students to think creatively and problem-solve in. My classroom is colorful and chock full of tools and resources. Students in my classroom room are taught to care for a variety of classroom pets, including various kinds of fish, a bearded dragon and a tarantula. They launch weather balloons, make models with a 3D printer, work with drones and robots, or film activities and presentations using a GoPro.

It is essential that students play a significant role in the process of their learning and can solve problems using what they know and have learned. By using critical thinking skills to collaborate and complete performance-based lessons, my students are fully engaged throughout the entire school year.

Giving up Control (i.e. Putting your ego in your pocket)

Occasionally teachers trying PBL will say to me, "My kids can't do it" or "It's a lot of work." I suspect the real issue here is teachers not wanting to give up control of their classroom. As educators, we have to change our approach to teaching. PBL allows student to take charge of their learning, which permits the teacher the freedom to facilitate and encourage critical thinking. Additionally, I find students work better when the teacher isn't hovering over them. PBL promotes creative thinking and builds the 21st-century skills pupils need to be successful in today's job market.

However, the school administrators must be on board with the concept for it to work efficiently. I recall getting an unannounced walk through from my principal. He remarked that what he observed was all fine, but he wanted to see more traditional teaching. I took issue with that statement. It really bothered me to the core. My students were working hard, collaborating, and problem-solving. Nonetheless, the principal emphasized his desire to see more traditional instruction. I respectfully shared with him that my students were performing at a very high level and I wanted to continue on the path I had taken. He marked up his rubric and again commented on the need for more conventional teaching. I adamantly disagreed and refused to sign that observation.

At the end of the year when test scores were released, his opinion about PBL changed. It is now mandatory for teaching to implement one unit per quarter.

Use a Pre-built, Credible, Standards-aligned Curriculum

I've discovered that Defined STEM is a great tool to help me create relevant career-connected lessons I can incorporate into Johnsonville. The supplementary curriculum provides students with research resources, videos, and project prompts that encourage students to think outside the box and put them in real-world situations. The curriculum grants maximum flexibility and makes it possible for me to change parts of the lesson to fit the specific needs of my classroom. It is a one-stop shop for PBL.

The Learning Space

My learning space is designed for three essential elements: collaboration, critical thinking, and citizenship. I strongly believe these are vital 21st-century skills students need to effectively compete in the global arena.

There is one rule that students learn when they enter my classroom – the desk in there is mine. I get upset if anyone touches it! That same principal applies to how students feel about their learning space. And you will find in my classroom that students take pride in their work areas. It is important that students take initiative and an active part in their learning. They also should be given the opportunity to solve problems using the information they have learned in Johnsonville.

Collaboration is the key!

In 2011, I was selected an Apple Distinguished Educator (ADE). I was honored to be the only one picked from the state of North Carolina. In July, I arrived in Phoenix, Arizona from the summer institute eager to prove why I was chosen. On the very first day, we were grouped at tables and were asked to complete a task together. I immediately thought to myself - I'm going to take charge and show the rest of the teachers how we should complete the challenge.

Before the ADE Alumni got started, there was only one rule to the challenge: "You cannot be a BUTT!" For a second, I felt like it was directed at me and felt kind of offended. I didn't appreciate anyone calling me a "butt." But after listening to the rest of his statement, it made total sense. He was saying, don't use the word "but" when you're engaged in doing a collaborative effort. Each of us had something of value to add in completing the task.

Using the word "and" was encouraged.

"But" was not allowed.

Today, I always make sure that the word "but" has no place in our collaborative tasks and that it is drafted into the classroom's constitution.

By using critical thinking skills to collaborate and complete performance-based lessons, I have found that students are fully engaged throughout the entire school year.

Technology Integration

I believe the power of technology to transform learning and the lives of my students has no limitations. Providing an iPad for every student allows more self-paced and individualized learning. The devices enable students to set appropriate learning goals, evaluate their progress, and helps them stay engaged with digital and multimedia materials. Students in 21st-century classrooms can create reports and presentations with graphics and images, preserve a spreadsheet to keep track of their grades, and maintain an electronic portfolio.

Creativity and writing skills are developed by creating movies of their interpretations of historical events and recording audio productions of stories and historical facts. Use, and even the creation of interactive electronic books is commonplace. Students are encouraged to check their iPad calendar for the daily agenda and assignments. These tasks encourage students to work collaboratively with other students. My students do all the tasks mentioned previously on a regular basis.

This past school year we used Wirecast for special projects like weather forecasting, ecosystems, and more. Currently, my students will be broadcasting a live newscast to the entire school. I'm sold on the capabilities of Wirecast because of the interface and ease of use. In the past, I had a S.W.A.T. Team (Students Working to Assist with Technology) that picked up on the software and ran the broadcast themselves. It takes no time for my students to learn the software and start using it on their own. When I was a technology facilitator I used the software weekly. In the classroom, my students use the software as needed.

Grow Your Professional Learning Network

One of the many benefits of being an Apple Distinguished Educator is working with the best minds in the teaching profession! Every summer for the past eight years, I have spent a week collaborating and creating content with outstanding teachers. What I learned from those experiences, I share with other educators via staff development, monthly tech talks with other teachers, my website, iTunes U courses, and social media sites to strengthen the profession. Collaborating and sharing with educators greatly enhances the teaching profession.

What good is it to teach innovation in isolation? Collaborating is pivotal for growth, not only for students but for educators as well. Six years ago, I launched the website www.teachthisway.com. The website has a strong following of teachers from across the country. The idea to create the site was born after I attended the Apple Academy at Apple in Cupertino, California. Apple chose 95 educators from across the country to come and learn how the iPad can transform learning. It turned out to be a life-changing experience for me. I learned so much from the teachers attending and the Apple staff that I quickly purchased the domain to create my site and began developing content immediately.

There is an immeasurable reward in sharing ideas and mentoring other educators. In addition to my website, I have authored several iTunes U courses and Multi-Touch books to serve in the same capacity. Currently there are over 1,000 teachers following me on Twitter. Some of the best ideas and concepts I learned about teaching were derived from other teachers. The best teachers are students first. In addition to www.teachthisway.com, my students and I collaborated with TED and launched http://johnsonvillelearningnetwork.com/. The site serves as a professional resource for teacher to continue their education.

Chapter 7

The Mini Funk Factory

In our contemporary society, it is still rare to see a male teacher in an elementary classroom. African American men are even a more unique sighting. In my school of more than 60 employees, only five are male. I believe this unquestionably has an impact on our male students; especially those without positive male role models in their homes. In spite of this, it affords men like me with a unique opportunity to reach out to these students and inspire them to accomplish great things in their lives – both in the classroom and in the community. We need to recognize that we have a responsibility and the power to prevent an achievement gap before it begins.

Long ago, I made a commitment to myself that I would devote my life to giving the youth in our community a chance to become successful in whatever way I could. One of the programs I created that offers possibilities for our youth to become successful is through the Salisbury Mini Funk Factory Marching Band https://www.minifunkfactory.org). I founded this nonprofit organization with the purpose of inspiring and empowering young people through music.

It started when I worked as the technology facilitator at Overton Elementary School. The School Improvement Team began discussing ways to improve the test scores of African American males. It was pretty much the same old unimaginative game plan as years before: buy some more books and a motivation poster or two. I started getting frustrated and finally spoke out. I proposed forming a drum circle for eight at-risk boys with the belief it would improve their focus in the classroom.

It was called the Mini Funk Factory band, but it didn't start out fully loaded with instruments. We began with eight students beating on buckets. Then we graduated to actual drums after I bought a drum set and took it apart and split up the drums among the students. At the time, I didn't have the manpower to start a large band, so that's why we created the small drum circle. Later down the line more drums started arriving and there was a rush of students asking to join. Three weeks later, the Overton Elementary School Mini Funk Factory drum-line amounted to 45 enthusiastic students!

I am so happy and proud to say, the experiment turned out to be a huge success. After several months of hard work, practicing and performing, the drumline swelled to 60 students and we expanded to a full marching band! Once the word spread about our marching band, monetary donations and instruments began arriving from all over the country. Livingstone College's marching band agreed to partner with us, and together, we hosted the FIRST-EVER elementary school band camp in Rowan County in 2011.

In 2013, the band created a partnership with the City of Salisbury to reach out and recruit more students in the area. Open enrollment was also offered to any elementary or middle school child in grades four through eight in Rowan County.

Its name was soon changed to the Salisbury Mini Funk Factory Marching Band. Today, we practice twice a week at Livingstone College and provide music instruction to students. Students in my program have performed in front of thousands of people across the state and at college football games as far away as Alabama. In 2012, the band performed in the Charlotte St. Patrick's Day parade where there were 90,000 people lining the streets yelling and screaming for the band. That's when I knew the program had grown. The kids were well prepared, displayed discipline, and were not all phased by the raucous crowd. I was so proud of them.

The marching band in June of 2016, played in Denver, Colorado, to represent the City of Salisbury at the All-American City Competition. Our student band is comprised of a vast economically disadvantaged population in the

Rowan-Salisbury School System. Studies have proven that these students enter school with significantly lower skills in the five major areas of development and learning compared to students in higher income families. Language skills were 38 percent lower and math skills were 37 percent less.

Is all of this change actually paying off?

I am delighted to reveal that we have witnessed remarkable and measurable success. At the end of the 2011-2012 school year, 70 percent of the students who were members of the Overton Mini Funk Factory passed their End-of Grade Test. Every year since the inception of the program The Mini Funk Factory, at least 70 percent of the students pass their End-of Grade Test.

What's more, North Carolina testing proves that my PBL model improves student scores. Comparatively, at the end of the 2016 school year, my 5th-grade students scored an average of 85 percent on the state science exam, while my school as a whole scored 58 percent. Without a doubt, I am able to conclusively state that my concentration on PBL and hands-on learning was the catalyst for this major boost in test scores.

As I discussed previously, my students not only have learned about what steps it takes to earn a "passing" grade; they have taken substantial strides toward how to function in society as successful working adults. I quote

Aristotle to them all the time: We are what we repeatedly do. Excellence then, is not an act, but a habit." I try to instill in my students that you're going to have to do it yourself. This world doesn't owe you anything. You're going to have to go out and get everything yourself.

Such life lessons are not exclusive to my interactions in the classroom, they are also prevalent in my home life, too. I have three daughters ages, 19, 17, and 15. I preach to them all the time about valuing education and insist that they study in school and listen. A lot of the bad experiences I dealt with in my life I try to shield them from. I don't cuss around them and I don't have them around people who cuss and act certain ways. On the other hand, I venture to give them experience I never had by taking them on a college campuses, taking them to see football games, and other endeavors.

While on a business trip in Germany, my senior daughter in high school was on a 14-day excursion through Europe. We ended up in Munich at the same time, which was quite an irony. I have obtained passports for all my daughters and taken trips with them outside of the United States. I feel that type of experience is invaluable because it exposes them to the world. They can see there is so much more to life than where they live.

Conclusion

It's weird for me to think that as a kid I had

no dreams, was usually inattentive in his classes,

and now I'm described by many of my students

and peers as a "dream maker," a person with a

"heart of gold," and a "light in the darkness." The

irony is, I rarely dreamed as a kid, but I dream now about opening the eyes of every kid I am in contact with and helping them to learn about what it takes for them to succeed.

I am tremendously grateful for all the wonderful recognition, love, and being lauded as transformative and non-conventional as a result of my work. However, even while I embrace these kudos and sentiment, I also remember that I promised myself to never become complacent or satisfied with the status quo.

It's not about the awards for me. I am here because of and for my students. The rewards for my work signify a further call for action. Such honors not only validate my efforts, but reignite my passion to impact the educational system on

an even grander scale.

Acknowledgements

It is by the grace of God that I am in this position today. Husband, father, teacher, mentor, and friend. I sincerely like to thank my wife, Desiree, who is a solid rock in my corner. Without your love and patients no way I would have made it this far. My daughters, Jessieca, Adanya and Kailah. Thank you for your love and support. My brothers and sister, Nello, Andrew, Phillip and Lisa, you guys always have my back, and I will forever have yours. My cousins, Carl, Lionell Jr, and George, you are my brothers!

I am thankful for Livingstone College, it was beneath thy maples and thy oaks I found my calling and purpose in life. Dr. Jimmy Jenkins, thank you for providing a home to the Mini Funk Factory Marching Band. It is your leadership and vision that is changing the lives of youth in our city. Thank you, Sidney Sessoms, former Director of Bands at Livingstone College and Anthony Jones, current Director of Bands at Livingstone College. The Mini Funk Factory would not be what it is today without your help.

To my brothers of the Gamma Delta chapter of Kappa Alpha Psi Fraternity, Inc. Thank you for holding me up to a high standard.

Thank you to Mr. Jerome Heggins my first principal at Isenberg Elementary School. Sir, I owe you my career. Without your leadership, Johnsonville would not exist! Thank you, Marvin Moore, my current principal. I know I pushed the limits. Thank you for allowing me the space to express myself.

Big thank you to PR with Panache and Julie Brolin! Words cannot express how grateful I am to you guys. Johnsonville is a world-wide name thanks to your work!

Thank you, Dr. Samantha Lacey! You, Hugh and Alana, are now family. I am grateful to have you as a mentor and friend.

Thank you, Dr. Wayne Wilson! Your hard work and help are much appreciated!

Philippians 4:13

I can do all this through him who gives me strength.

58566491R10083

Made in the USA
Columbia, SC
23 May 2019